Voice/Piano/Guitar

CONTENTS

THE WIND BENEATH MY WINGS

4
Eb(add F)
Bb/D
Cm7
3fr.
face.
You were con-
Fsus4
F
tent to let___ me___ shine, that's your way,___
Cm7
3fr.
Fsus4
you al-ways walked the step___ be - hind.
F
Bb
Eb/Bb
Bb
So, I___ was the one with all___ the
It might___ have ap-peared to go___ un-

Eb(add F)
Bb
glo - ry,
no - ticed,
while you ___ were the
but I've ___ got it
Eb/Bb
Bb
Eb(add F)
Gm7
one with all ___ the strength.
all here in ___ my heart.
Cm7
Bb/C
Fsus4
A beau-ti-ful face with-out ___ a name ___
I want you to know I know ___ the truth, ___
of
F
Cm7
Bb/C
Cm7
for so long, ___
course I know ___ it,
a beau-ti-ful smile to hide ___ the
I ___ would be noth-ing with-out

Fsus4
F
D7/F#
x 0
Gm7
3fr.
pain.
you.
Did you ev - er know
F/Eb
Eb
Bb
F/A
0
that you're my he - ro,
Gm7
3fr.
F/Eb
Eb
Bb
and ev - 'ry - thing I would like to be?
F/A
0
F
D/F#
x 0
Gm7
3fr.
F/Eb
Eb
I can fly high - er than an

Bb
F/A
Gm7
Cm7
To Coda
ea - gle,
'cause you are the
Fsus4
F
1.
Bb(add C)
wind   be - neath   my   wings.
D.S. al Coda
Eb(add F)
2.
Bb
Eb/Bb
Bb
F/A
wings.
Coda
Bb/F
F
Bb(add C)
wind   be - neath   my   wings.

Eb(add F)/Bb
Bbsus2
F7sus4/Eb
Bb(add C)
Bb/D
F7sus4/Eb
F/A
Bbsus2
Fly,
fly,
fly a - way, you let
me fly so high. Oh, fly,

F7sus4/Bb
Eb
Bb
G
F
fly,
so
Bb(add C)
Bb/D
F7sus4/Eb
high a - gainst the sky,
so high I al - most touch
F/A
Bb(add C)
the sky.
Thank you,
thank you,
thank
Eb/Bb
Fsus4
Bb(add C)
God for you,
the wind be - neath my
wings.

LET THE RIVER RUN
(Theme from "Working Girl")

Words and Music by
CARLY SIMON

lights, ________ the streets there meet ________ them, and si - rens call them
on with a song.
It's ask - ing for the
tak - ing, trem - bling, shak - ing. ___
Ah, ________ my heart is ach - ing. We're com - ing to the edge, run - ning on the wa - ter;
A F#m E D F#m E A5 A F#m B/D# D(addE) 2fr. A/C# F#m G E E/D

12
C#m7
E/B
C
F/C
com- ing through the fog, your sons and daugh- ters.
Sing the great - est song, stand on a
(Instrumental)
C
Am
G
F
Am
G
star and blaze a trail____ of de - sire through the dark near____
C5
C
To Coda
Am
D/F#
dawn.
It's ask - ing for the tak - ing. Come
It's
Fsus2
C/E
run with me now, the sky is the col- or of blue; you've nev- er e- ven seen in the eyes of a

Am
Bb
G
G/F
lov- er.____ My heart is ach - ing. We're com- ing to the edge, run - ning on the wa - ter;
Em7
G/D
D.S. al Coda
Coda
Am
D/F#
com- ing through the fog, your sons and daugh- ters
ask - ing for the tak - ing,
F(addG)
C/E
Am
trem - bling, shak - ing.__ Ah,__________ my heart is
Bb
G
G/F
ach - ing. We're com- ing to the edge, run - ning on the wa - ter;

Em7   G/D   C
com- ing through the fog, your sons and daugh - ters. Let the riv - er
F/C   C   Am   G
run, let all the dream - ers wake the na - tion.
F   Am   G   C
Come, the new Je - ru - sa - lem.
Repeat and fade
C

THE BATMAN THEME
From the Motion Picture BATMAN™

molto legato
mf
f
p
ff
p
mf
f
p
ff
p
mf
(non legato)

8va
mp
8va
loco
(R.H.)
R.H.
mf
loco
(R.H.)
R.H.
mf
f
mf
ff
marcato

STAR WARS
(Main Theme)
From the Motion Pictures "STAR WARS", "THE EMPIRE STRIKES BACK" &
"RETURN OF THE JEDI"
A Lucasfilm Ltd. Production – A Twentieth Century-Fox Release

Music by
JOHN WILLIAMS

STAND BY ME

Words and Music by
BEN E. KING, MIKE STOLLER
and JERRY LEIBER
Slowly
When the night has come and the land is dark And the moon is the on-ly light we'll see, No, I won't be a-fraid, no I

LA BAMBA

Moderate "Latin Rock" beat

Adaptation and Arrangement by
RITCHIE VALENS

Am
F
won't   be a - fraid   Just as long_______ as you
G7
C
stand,_________ Stand By Me.   So, dar - ling, dar - ling,
C
Am
Stand___   By   Me,   oh,___   Stand___   By Me,   Oh,
F
G7
C
stand,________   Stand By Me,   Stand By Me._______
mf
Fine

C
Am
If the sea________ that we look up-on should tum-ble and fall Or the
F
G7
C
moun-tain________ should crum-ble________ in the sea, I won't
Am
cry, I won't cry, no________ I__ won't shed a tear Just as
F
G7
C
D. S. al Fine
long________ as you stand,________ Stand By Me. So, dar-ling, dar-ling,
mp

LA BAMBA

Adaptation and Arrangement by
RITCHIE VALENS
Moderate "Latin Rock" beat
mf
C F G7 C F G7
C F G7 C F G7
Pa - ra bai - lar la Bam - ba. Pa - ra bai - lar la Bam-
C F G7 C F G7
ba se ne - ce - si - ta un po - ca de gra - cia.
C F G7
Un - a po - ca de gra - cia para mi para ti y ar - ri - ba ar - ri-

C F G7 C F G7
ba; ar - ri - ba ar - ri - ba por ti se re__
C F G7
__ por ti se re se re. Yo no soy mar - i -
C F G7 C F G7
ne - ro. Yo no soy mar - i - ne - ro, soy cap - i - tan:__
C F G7
__ yo no soy mar - i - ne - ro, soy cap - i - tan.__
To Coda

C   F   G7   C   F   G7
Bam - ba____ bam-ba,   bam - ba____ bam-
C   F   G7
ba,   bam - ba,____ bam - ba,
C   F   G7   D.S. al Coda
bam - ba____ bam...__ Pa - ra bai - lar____ la bam-
Repeat and fade
Coda   C   F   G7
Bam - ba,____ bam - ba!

CHARIOTS OF FIRE

From the ENIGMA PRODUCTION, LADD COMPANY/WARNER BROS. Release
"CHARIOTS OF FIRE"

Composed by
VANGELIS

Fm Gb Db
Fm Ab7 Db
Fm Gb Db Gb/Ab
Db
Fm Gb Db
Fm Ab7 Db
Fm Gb Db Gb/Ab
Db Gb/Db
Fm Gb Db Ab7
Db Gb/Db
D.S. al Coda
CODA
Db Gb/Db
Db Gb/Db
Db Gb/Db
Db Gb/Db
Db Gb/Db
Db Gb/Db
Db Gb/Db
Db Gb/Db
Db

SEPARATE LIVES
(Love Theme From "WHITE NIGHTS")

Words and Music by
STEPHEN BISHOP

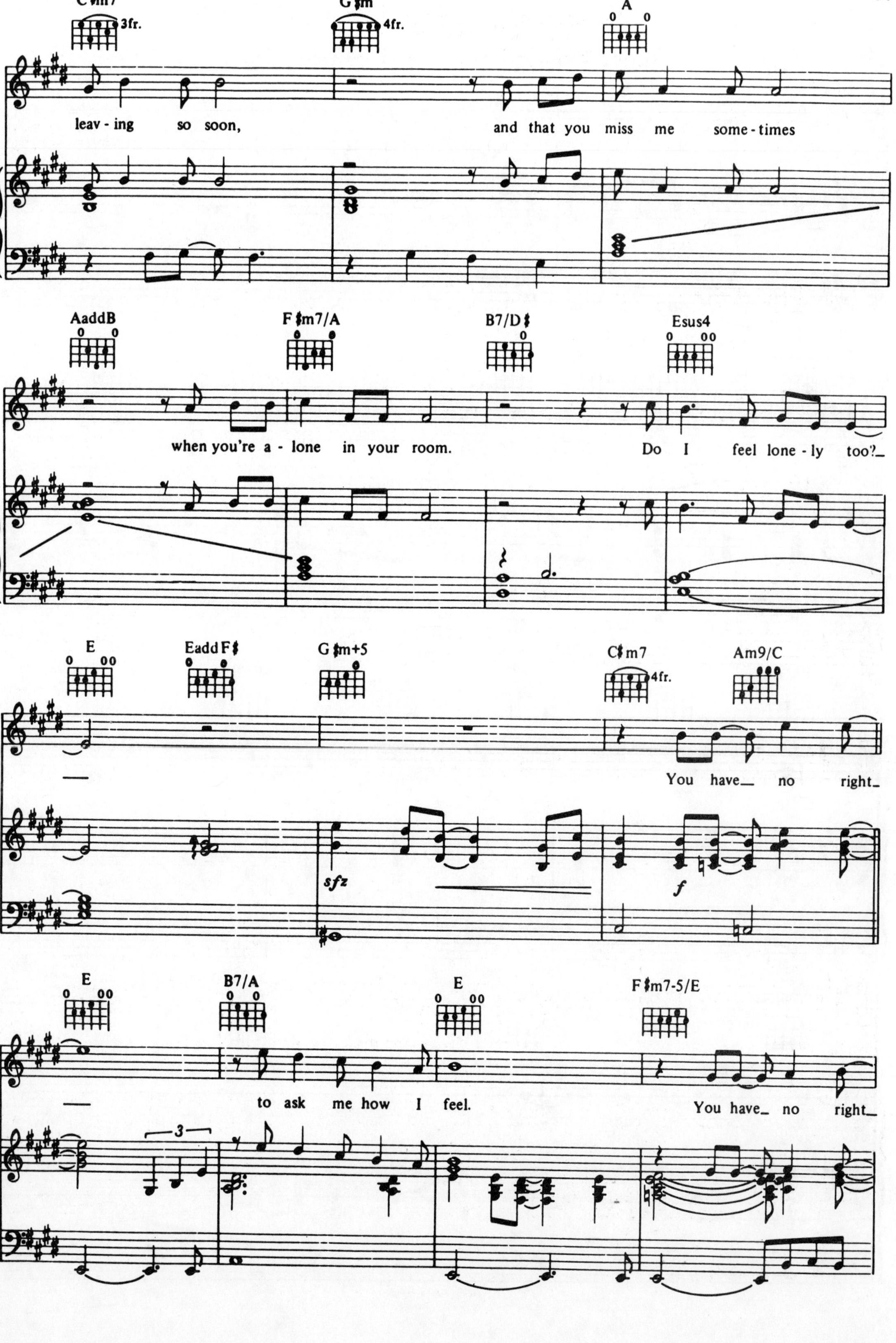
C♯m7
3fr.
G♯m
4fr.
A
leav - ing so soon,
and that you miss me some - times
AaddB
F♯m7/A
B7/D♯
Esus4
when you're a - lone in your room.
Do I feel lone - ly too?
E
Eadd F♯
G♯m+5
C♯m7
4fr.
Am9/C
You have no right
sfz
f
E
B7/A
E
F♯m7-5/E
to ask me how I feel.
You have no right
3

E
F#m7/A
B7
to speak to me so kind.
A/C# G#m/B F#m/C# E/G# A
Bm7sus4
B7
I can't go on just hold-ing on to ties.
C#m7sus4
C#m7 4fr.
G#m7 4fr.
E/G#
F#m7
3
now that we're liv-ing
3
mf
B7sus4 2fr.
E
A/E
sep - 'rate lives.
3
3

Well, I held on
to let you go
and if you lost your love for me
will you nev-er let it show.
There was no way

A
B7sus4
B7
C#m7sus4
C#m7
G#m7
E/G#
to com - pro - mise
so now we're
F#7
B7sus4
E
liv - ing
sep - 'rate lives.
AaddB
G#m7+5
F#7
C#m7/G#
AaddB/E
Ooo,
it's so ty - pi - cal
love leads to is - o - la - tion.
F#m7
G#m+5
A
So you build that wall,
yes, you build that wall
E/G#

B7sus4
C#m7
D9
A6 B7sus4/G#
and you make it strong-er.
Well, you have no right
E
B7/A
E
F#m7-5/E
to ask me how I feel.
You have no right
E
F#m7/A
B7
to speak to me so kind.
A/C#
G#m
F#m7
E
A
Freely
Some-day I might find my-self
subito mf
ff

Bm7sus4
B7
E
G#m7
F#m7
look - ing in__ your eyes,
but for now we'll go 'on liv-
B7
E
F#m7
C#m7
Freely
ing sep - 'rate lives.
Yes, for now we'll go on
mp
rit.
mf
F#m7-5/C
B7-9
C#m7
AaddB
E
liv - ing sep - 'rate lives.
Ha ha ha
mf a tempo
AaddB/E
G#m+5
F#m7/A
B7sus4
E
ha.___ Ha ha ha__ ha ha. Sep - 'rate lives.
molto rit.

BURNING HEART
From the Original Motion Picture Soundtrack ROCKY IV

Words and Music by
JIM PETERIK and FRANKIE SULLIVAN

C/G   G   C/E   Am   G   Fmaj7
so much at stake___ seems our free-dom's up a-gainst the ropes.___ Does the
you a-gainst you___ it's the par-a-dox that drives us all.___ It's a

G/F   Fmaj7   G/F
crowd un-der-stand?___ Is it east ver-sus west or man a-gainst man?___ Can
mat-ter of wills___ in the heat of at-tack it's the pas-sion that kills.___ The

F   G/F   Fmaj7   G/F   G   Am   F/A
an-y na-tion stand___ a-lone.
vic-to-ry is yours___ a-lone.
In the burn-ing heart

f

G/A   Am   F/A   G/A   Am/E   G
just a-bout to___ burst there's a quest for an-swers and a bridge of the past.___

Am
F
G
F/C G/B Am
F
G Am
in the dark-est night   ris-ing like a spi - re   in the burn-ing heart the un-mis- tak-a-ble fire...
1.
F/A G/A   F
2.
N.C.
_ In the burn-- ing heart._
In the _
mf
ff
D.S. al Coda
sfz
Repeat and fade
(Am)
F/A
G/A Am
F/A
G/A
Coda
In the burn-ing   heart._
mf

PACHELBEL CANON IN D

41
mf
mp
mp
mf
mf
mp
mf

f
cresc.
ff
cresc.
ff

CAN YOU READ MY MIND?
(Love Theme from "SUPERMAN")
A WARNER BROS. film

Words by
LESLIE BRICUSSE

Music by
JOHN WILLIAMS

Bbm7   Eb7sus4   Abmaj7   Eb/Db   Db   Eb/Db   Db
hands_____ with a god or a fool. Will you look at me quiv - er - ing like a
Db/Cb   Cb   Db/Cb   Cb   Fm7   Gm7   Abmaj7   Bb7
lit - tle girl shiv - er - ing. You can see right through me.
Eb   F7/Eb   Fm7   Bb7sus4   Bb7   Eb   Bb7sus4
Can you read my mind? Can you pic - ture the things I'm think - ing of?_____
Eb   F7/Eb   Abm7
Won - d'ring why you are all the won - der - ful things you

Bb7sus4   Bb7   Bbm7   Eb7sus4   Abmaj7
are.   You can fly.______ You be-long to the sky.   You and
Bbm7   Eb7sus4   Fm7-5   Bb7   Eb   F7/Eb
I______ could be-long to each oth - er.   If you need a friend,
Fm7   Gm7   Ab   Fm7   Bb7sus4   Bb7   Eb   Abmaj7
I'm   the   one   to   fly   to.   If you need   to be
Eb   Abmaj7   Am7-5   Cm/D   G
loved,   here I am.   Read   my   mind!______

THE THORN BIRDS THEME
From The Warner Bros. T.V. Movie "THE THORN BIRDS"

By
HENRY MANCINI

Gm/F
F
C/F
F
Bb
C/Bb
F/A
Dm
Gm 3fr.
Gm/C 3fr.
F
Bb
C/Bb
F/A
Dm
Gm 3fr.
Gm/C 3fr.
F
3
3
Gm/F
F
C/F
F
Gm/F
F
Bb/F
Bb/C
F
molto rit.

SEND IN THE CLOWNS

Bb/Eb   Fm/Eb   Eb   Gm   Dm7
clowns?   Send in the clowns.   Just when I'd stopped   op-en-ing
Gm   Dm9   Gm
doors,   Fin-al-ly   know-ing the one that I want-ed was
Cm7   G   Eb6/Bb   F7/A   Ab6
yours,   Mak-ing my   en-trance a-gain with my u-su-al
Gsus4   Fm7(-5)   Gm/Bb   Ab6/Bb   Bb/Eb   Ab
flair,   Sure of my lines,   No one is there.
poco rit.

Bb/Eb
Ab
Eb
Ebsus4
Eb
Ebmaj9
Don't you love farce?
rich,
My fault, I fear.
Is - n't it queer,
I thought that
Los - ing my
a tempo
poco rit.
Eb
Abmaj9
Ab6
Bb13/Eb
you'd want what I want. Sor - ry, my dear.
tim - ing this late in my ca - reer?
But where are the clowns?
And where are the clowns?
Quick, send in the
There ought to be
1. Bb9/Eb
Eb
Ebsus4
Eb
Ebsus4
clowns.
Don't both - er, they're here.
Is - n't it
2. Bb9/Eb
Eb
Ebsus4
Eb
clowns.
Well, may - be next year...
poco rit.
a tempo
ten.
rit.

JESSICA'S THEME
(Breaking In The Colt)
From "THE MAN FROM SNOWY RIVER"

Composed and Arranged by
BRUCE ROWLAND

A
Bm
G
D
1 Asus 4
A
2 Asus 4
A
F
C7
C7
A7
Dm
1 A
2 A
D.S. al

Asus 4
A
D
G
Asus 4
A7
D
8ve
G
Asus 4
A7
loco.
A#o
Bm
R.H.
G
Asus 4
D
A
G
8ve
16ve
D
8va lower

SONG FROM M*A*S*H
(Suicide Is Painless)

1. Try to find a way to make
All our little joys relate
Without that ever-present hate
But now I know that it's too late.
    And, Chorus

3. The game of life is hard to play,
I'm going to lose it anyway,
The losing card I'll someday lay,
So this is all I have to say,
    That: Chorus

4. The only way to win, is cheat
And lay it down before I'm beat,
And to another give a seat
For that's the only painless feat.
    'Cause: Chorus

5. The sword of time will pierce our skins,
It doesn't hurt when it begins
But as it works it's way on in,
The pain grows stronger, watch it grin.
    For: Chorus

6. A brave man once requested me
To answer questions that are key,
Is it to be or not to be
And I replied; "Oh, why ask me."
    'Cause: Chorus

LEAN ON ME
(From The Original Motion Picture Soundtrack "Lean On Me")

Words and Music by
BILL WITHERS

A
D
D
there's_ al-ways to-mor - row._ Lean on me when you're not strong_
G
D
D/A
A
_ and I'll_ be_your friend,_ I'll help you car - ry on._ For I know_
Bm7
Em7
D/A
A
_ that it won't be long ____ 'til I'm gon-na need ___ some-bod-y to lean_
D
D
G
____ on._ Please, ___ swal-low your pride if I have

D   D/A   A   Bm7   Em7
things___ you need to bor - row.___ For no one, no one can fill___
Solo
Choir   D/A   A
                   all of your needs ___   if you wan- na let them
No one can fill. ___   Let___
Solo   D   No Chord   D   G
show.   Ad lib: You just call on me, brother, if you feel you need a hand.'Cause we all
Choir
___ them show.   Call me.___   We all

need somebody to lean on. I just might have a problem
need some-bod-y to lean ___ on. You call me.
you understand. Both: We all need some-bod-y to lean ___ on. Lean on me
Solo: when you're not strong. ___ And I'll be your ___ friend, ___ I'll help you car-
D A D N.C. N.C.
G Em7 D/A Bm7 A D
G D Bm/A

64
A
Bm7
Em7
ry on.___ For I __ know it won't be long _____ 'till I'm gon-na need__
Dm/A
A
D
N.C.
some - bod- y, some-bod- y to lean ___________ on. ____ Solo: You can
D
G
D
N.C.
SOLO:
call on me, sister, if you need a hand. We all need somebody to lean
CHOIR:
Call me.___ We all need some-bod- y to lean_

D   N.C.
D   G
on.   I just might have   a problem that   you can understand.   We all
Choir:
Oo. _____   Just call _ me.   We all
on.
D/A   Bm7   A   D
need   somebody   to   lean   on.
need   some - bod - y   lean   on. _____
D   G   D   G

D
G
D
Solo: If there is a load ___ you have to bear ___ that you can't
D/A
A
Bm7
Em7
car - ry, just re-mem- ber I, _____ I'm right up the road...
D/A
A
D
3
3
___ I'll ___ share your load _ if you just call me.
3
Repeat and fade
Em/D
D
Em/D
D
Vocal solo ad-lib.
Choir: (Call me. Call me. _____)

THAT'S WHAT FRIENDS ARE FOR

Fm7
Dm7(no 5th)
G7sus4
G7
well, then close your eyes___ and try___ to feel the way___ we do___ to - day,___
well, then close your eyes___ and know___ these words are com - ing from___ my heart,___

Cm7
Ab maj7
Fm7/Bb
Bb11
and then if you can___ re - mem - ber.___

Eb add9
Eb add9/D
Ab maj7/C
Bb/Ab
Keep smil - ing, keep shin - ing, know - ing you___ can al - ways count on
f

Gm7
Cm7
Ab maj7
Fm7/Bb
Bb9
me___ for sure___ that's what friends___ are for.

Ebadd9
Ebadd9/D
Db6(no 5th)
C7sus4
C7
For good - times and bad times
in good - times, in bad times
I'll be on your side for - ev - er
Cb6(no 5th)
Bb7sus4
1. Bb7sus4
To Coda
more.
That's what friends are for
2. Bb7sus4
D.S. al Coda
Coda
Bb7sus4
for.
for.
Repeat and fade
Vocal ad lib.
Ebmaj9
Ebmaj9/D
Ab(add Bb)/C
Gm7
Cm7
Fm7
Bb11

TWO HEARTS
From The Original Motion Picture Soundtrack "Buster"

Words by
PHIL COLLINS

Music by
LAMONT DOZIER

G   A/G   G
There was no rea-son to be-lieve___ she'll al-ways
(See additional lyrics)
A/G   G   A/G
be there.___ But if you don't put faith in what you be-
G   A/G   Am9
lieve in, it's get-ting no - where.__ 'Cause it
Bm7   Cmaj7   D7sus4   Am9
helps, you nev-er give up,___ don't look down,___ just look up.__

Bm7
Cmaj7
D7sus4
'Cause she's al - ways there be - hind you, just to re - mind you.
Cmaj7 C6
D
G
3
Two hearts liv - ing in just one mind. You know we're
Beat - ing to -
Cmaj7 C6
D
G
1.
two hearts liv - ing in just one mind.
geth - er 'til the end of time.
2.
Cmaj7 C6
3
You know we're two hearts liv - ing in

just one mind,_ to-geth-er for-ev-er_____
'til the end of time._
She knows_ there'll al-ways be a

74
D#7sus4
G#m7
4fr.
spe - cial place in my heart for her,
A#m7
G#/A#
Bmaj7
she knows, she knows, she knows. Yeah, she knows
G#m7
4fr.
A#m7
D#7sus4
no mat - ter how far a - part we are,
G#m7
4fr.
Am7
0 0 0
she knows
I'm al - ways right
3

Additional Lyrics

Well there's no easy way to, to understand it.
There's so much of my life in her
And it's like I planned it.
And it teaches you to never let go,
There's so much love you'll never know.
She can reach you no matter how far,
Wherever you are.

THE WAY WE WERE

Words by
ALAN and MARILYN BERGMAN

Music by
MARVIN HAMLISCH

Moderately slow

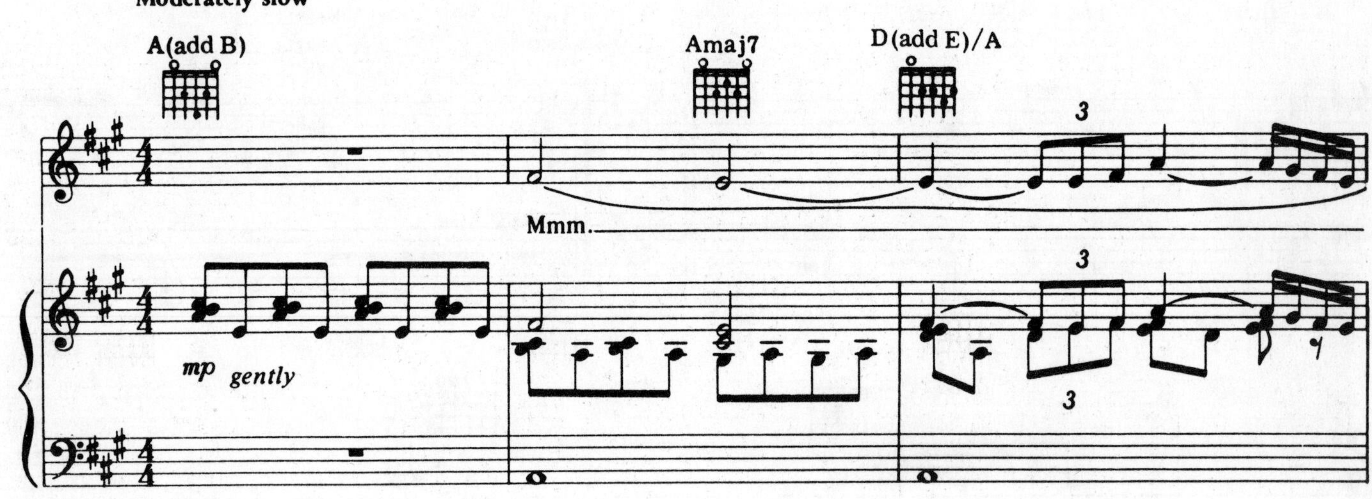

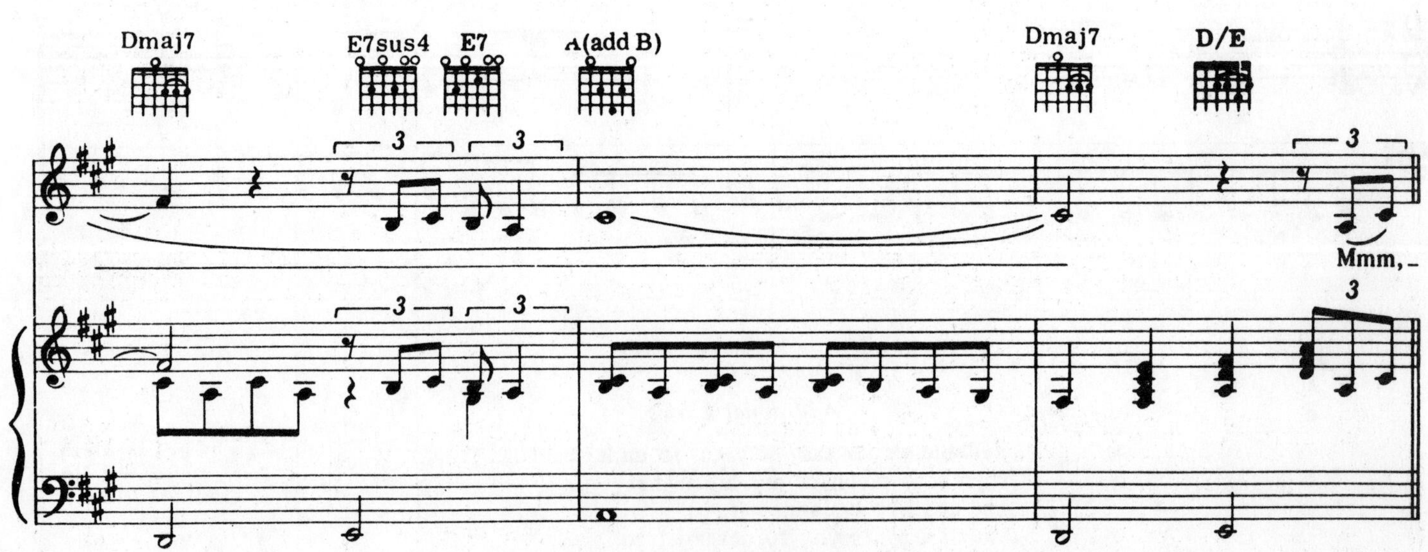

A(add B)
Amaj7
D(add E)/A
F#m(add G#)
F#m/E
mem - 'ries ______ light the cor - ners of my mind,
pic - tures ______ of the smiles ___ we left be - hind,
Dmaj7
C#7
F#sus4
F#m/E
Dmaj7
E7sus4
E7
mist - y wa - ter-col - or mem - 'ries ______ of the way we
smiles we give to one an - oth - er ______ for the way we
1.
A(add B)
Amaj7
Dmaj7
D/E
were. ______
2.
A(add B)
Amaj7
A9
Scat - tered were. ______
Dmaj7
C#m7
Bm7
C#m7
Can it be ___ that it was all so sim - ple then,
or has time __ re - writ - ten ev - 'ry
mf

F#9sus4
F#9
Bm7
Bm(maj7)
E7sus4
E7
line? If we had the chance to do it all a-gain, tell me
Amaj7
D/E
E7
A(add B)
Amaj7
D(add E)
would we? Could we? Mem - 'ries may be beau-ti-ful and
F#9sus4
F#m/E
Dmaj7
C#7
F#sus4
F#m/E
yet, what's too pain-ful to re - mem - ber,
Dmaj7
C#sus4 C#
F#m7
F#m7/E
Dmaj7
C#m7
we sim-ply choose to for - get. So it's the laugh - ter

79
Dmaj7
C#m7
Dmaj7
we will re - mem - ber, whenever we re-
C#m7
Bm7
E7sus4
A(add B)
Amaj7
mem - ber the way we were,
p
Dmaj9
A(add B)
Amaj7
the way we were. Mmm.
D(add E)/A
F#m(add G#)
F#m
Dmaj7
E7(add A)/D
Amaj9
3
3
rit.

A GROOVY KIND OF LOVE

Words and Music by
TONI WINE and
CAROLE BAYER SAGER

Bm7
C
D
heart beat, I can hear you breath - ing ___ in ___ my ___ ear.}
shiv - er, can't con-trol the quiv - er - ing ___ in - side}
Would-n't you a -
G
D/G
1. G
D
gree, ba - by, you and me got a groo-vy kind of love.
An - y - time you
2. G
D/G
A
E/A
love.
Oh. ___
mf
A
E/A
A
Bm/A

82
Bm7
C#m7
4fr.
D(addE)
2fr.
When I'm feel - in'
A
E/A
A
blue, all I got to do is take a look at you, then I'm not so___
Bm/A
Bm7
C#m7
4fr.
___ blue. When you're in my arms, noth - ing seems to mat - ter, my whole world could
D
E
A
shat - ter, I don't_ care._ Would-n't you a - gree,_ ba - by, you and
mp
mf
L.H.
L.H.

E/A
A
E/A
me got a groo-vy kind of love.
We got a groo-vy kind of_
A
E/A
D(addE)/F#
love.
We got a groo-vy kind of love.
E7sus4
D(addE)/F#
E7sus4
Wo.
D(addE)/F#
E7sus4
E7
A
We got a groo-vy kind of love.
mp rit.

LIVE TO TELL

Words and Music by
MADONNA CICCONE and PAT LEONARD

Dm C F Gm7 F
Some - times it gets so hard to hide it well.
I've seen it once, I know the warmth she gives.
C Dm C F
I was not
The light that
Gm7 F C Dm
read - y for the fall.
you could nev - er see.
Too
It
C F Gm7 F C
blind to see the writ - ing on the wall.
shines in - side, you can't take that from me.
85

Gm7/F
F
A man can tell a thou-sand lies, I've
Gm7/F
Am
Bb
Gm7/F
F
learned my les-son well. Hope I live to tell the se-cret I
Dm7
C/E
Dm7
C
have learned, 'till then it will burn in-side of me
1.
Bb
C
2.
Bb
C
Dm11
10fr.

Gm7/F
F
The truth is nev - er far_ be - hind,_ you
Gm7/F
Am
B♭
Gm7/F
F
kept it hid - den well._ If I live to tell _ the se - cret I_
Dm7
C/E
Dm7
C
_ knew then,_ will I
ev - er have the chance_ a - gain?_
B♭
C
Dm(no 3rd)

Slowly
Dm11
A tempo
No chord
Bb
C
If I ran a-way,__ I'd nev - er have__ the strength__
Dm7
Am7
Bb
to go ver - y far.__ How would they hear__ the beat-
C
Am7
Bb
ing of__ my heart?__ Will it grow cold,__

Bbmaj7
C
Dm7
the se - cret that_ I hide,_ will I grow old?_
Am7
Bb
C(addD)
How will they hear,_ when will they learn,_ how will they
Dm
C
F
know?_
Gm7
F
C
D.S. % (second ending and fade)

THEME FROM "SUPERMAN"

A WARNER BROS. film

By
JOHN WILLIAMS

3
3
3
3
3
3
3
3
cresc.
3
3
3
3
cresc.
(♩.♩.)
mf
cresc.
f

THE ROSE
From The Twentieth Century-Fox Motion Picture "THE ROSE"

Words and Music by
AMANDA McBROOM

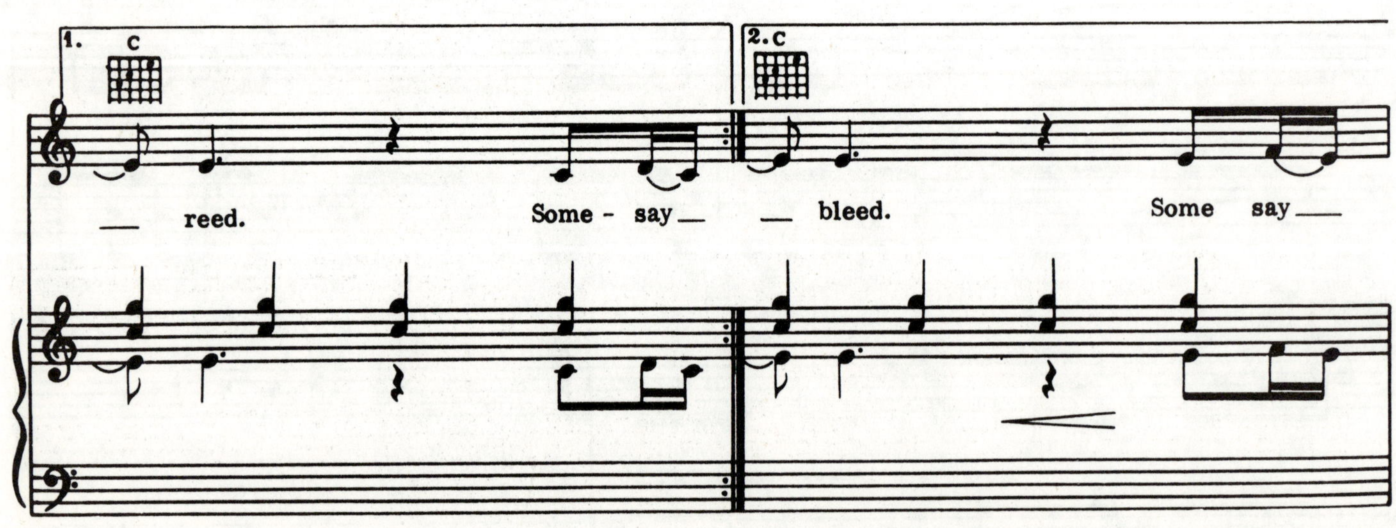

Cmaj7
F
(add 9)
F
love ___ it is a hun - ger ___ an end - less ach - ing
mf
G7sus
G7
C
G
need. ___ I say ___ love it is a flow - er ___ and
poco rit. - - - - - -
a tempo
F
C
you it's on - ly seed. ___ It's the ___
poco cresc.

96
G
F
G
heart a - fraid of break - ing that nev - er learns to
night has been too lone - ly and the road has been too
mf-f
C
G
dance. It's the dream a - fraid of wak - ing that
long, and you think that love is on - ly for the
F
G
C
Em
(B Bass)
Em
nev - er takes the chance. It's the one who won't
luck - y and the strong, just re - mem-ber in the
f
Am7
(G Bass)
Am7
F
G
be tak - en who can - not seem to give, and the
win-ter far be - neath the bit - ter snows lies the
rit. mf

C   G   1. F   G
soul   a - fraid of   dy - in'   that   nev - er ______   learns to
seed   that with the   sun's ___ love   in the
a tempo   cresc.
C
live. _______________________________   When the ___
f
2. F   G   C
spring   be - comes the   rose.
mf   rit.   a tempo
play 3 times   rit........

MISS CELIE'S BLUES (Sister)
From the Warner Bros. Motion Picture THE COLOR PURPLE

Words by
QUINCY JONES, ROD TEMPERTON
and LIONEL RICHIE

Music by
QUINCY JONES and ROD TEMPERTON

Slow and bluesy, 'gut-bucket' style

G7
C
B7
(Sung:) Sis - ter, __________ you've been on my mind, __
Em7-5/Bb
A7
D9   4fr.
sis - ter, __________ we're two of a kind, __ so sis - ter, __________ I'm
G7
C
C#°7   3fr.
G7
keep - in' my eye __ on you. __ I bet - cha think I don't know
C
B7
Em7-5/Bb
noth - in' __________ but sing - in' the blues, __ oh, sis - ter, __________ have

A7   D9   Ab7   G7+5
I got news for you; I'm some - thin'. _____ I hope you think that you're some-thin' too. _____
C   E7+5   Am   E7/B
Scuf - flin', _________ I been
Am/C   E7/B   Am   F7   Am   E7+5
up that lone-some road _____ and I seen a lot of suns go-in' down, _____ oh, _____ but
Am   E7/B   Am/C   A7/C#   D7   Ab7
trust me, no _____ low life's gon-na run me a - round.

G7
C
B7
So let me tell you some-thin'; sis - ter re - mem-ber your name, no
Em 7-5/Bb
A7
D7
twist-er gon-na steal your stuff a-way; my sis - ter, we
Ab7
G7+5
C
E7+5
A7
sho' ain't got a whole lot of time, so shake your shim - my,
D7
Ab7
G7
Freely
Rubato
C
G7+5
C7
sis - ter, 'cus hon-ey, the shug is feel - in' fine!

CAVATINA
(From "THE DEER HUNTER")

By
STANLEY MYERS

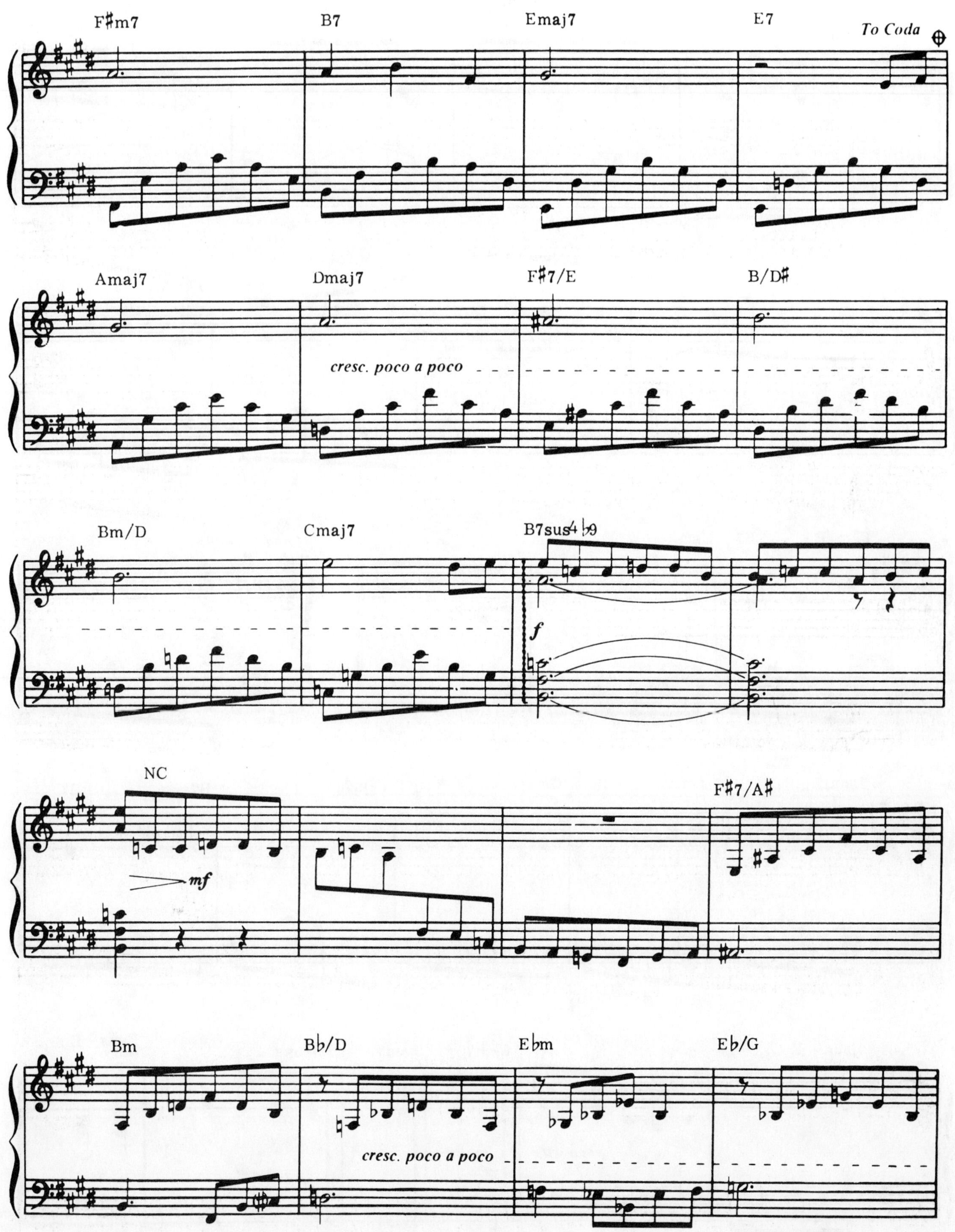
F#m7
B7
Emaj7
E7
To Coda
Amaj7
Dmaj7
F#7/E
B/D#
cresc. poco a poco
Bm/D
Cmaj7
B7sus4 b9
f
NC
F#7/A#
mf
Bm
Bb/D
Ebm
Eb/G
cresc. poco a poco

G#m
E
B7
E7
A
F#m7
F#m/B
B7
Esus4
E
D.C. al Coda
Coda
Amaj7
Dmaj7
Gmaj7
Cmaj7
F#m7
B7sus4
B7
Esus4
E
C#m7
F#m7
B9sus4
Esus4 E
(add 9)
mf
poco rit.
molto rit.